GRIEF

Decoding Fear Based Emotions

Net-Hetep Ta'Nesert

#BeeInspired Publishing

OKLAHOMA CITY, OKLAHOMA

#BeeInspired Publishing
Oklahoma City, Oklahoma 73120
www.beeinspiredpublishing.com

Publisher's Note: This is a work of fiction. Names, characters, places, and incidents are a product of the author's imagination. Locales and public names are sometimes used for atmospheric purposes. Any resemblance to actual people, living or dead, or to businesses, companies, events, institutions, or locales is completely coincidental.

Grief/ Net-Hetep Ta'Nesert. -- 1st ed.
ISBN 978-1-9487253-4-3
Grief/ Net-Hetep Ta'Nesert. – 2nd ed.
ISBN 978-1-948752-45-9

GETTING **R**EAL INFORMATION ELIMINATES FEAR –

DISCOVER THE SCIENCES BEHIND FEAR BASED EMOTIONS

Dedicated to Humanity

GRIEF

Look up any definition and it will describe as well as define the word grief as something emotionally overwhelming that involves sadness, loss, and suffering, accompanied by a sense of feeling numb to life.

Many doctors and other professionals operating within the Grief Management Industry, warn their clients to prepare themselves for varying levels of anguish, remorse, bitterness, and guilt, along with other recognized symptoms associated with grief. Persons facing grief have no set time limits for their 'mourning' periods because grief is different for each person experiencing it.

Humanity knows that whether it is man and or beast Grief is both personal and universal.

I say, "It's Time to Decode Grief and Discover the Sciences behind Fear Based Emotions".

Dedicated to all of us with a driven purpose to assist us in finally understanding, how we can heal our broken hearts when we have an understanding of the science behind fear-based emotions.

Net-Hetep Ta'Nesert, CGO

GRIEF

What scary, beastly, and monstrous images along with legions of haunting definitions instantly enter into your thoughts when you give this word life? Does speaking the spellbinding equation of this mystical 5-letter beast, immediately transport you into its hellish labyrinth? Medical Physicians, Psychologists and Grief Experts have identified the first 5 hideous companions of Grief that we all are destined to face. They are lurking within our emotions.

There are numerous descriptions, theorized concepts, debatable sciences and professions specializing in informing us about what 'e'motional components *'Grief'* sumptuously thrives on.

Is **"FEAR"** the wicked Ruler and Chief orchestrator of these emotionally debilitating, scary beasts?

Science and all religious systems use and talk about the significance of numbers. Everything in life is a living equation of a group of numbers whose sum total can give us a greater insight into the deeper meanings of the origins of various illnesses; and dis-eases.

Even the very moment, minute, hour, month, day, and date associated with the causes of humanity's grief, relates to the sum of individual numbers. The day, date and time of your

5

conception along with how many tri (3) mesters will elapse determining the month and date of your anticipated arrival is associated with numbers. Celebrations, marriages, divorces, and calamities along with the time, date, and day we die all relate to a group of numbers!

The unexpected experience of having to detach from persons and things of significant importance in our lives, places our hearts into mental spaces filled immediately with shock. Confusion, uncertainty, and "Fear" soon release destabilizing, hormonal chemicals into anatomical systems meant to keep our bodies in balance. After experiencing an overdose of these chemicals without **'G'**etting any **'R'**eal **'I'**nformation meant to provide sufficient answers to **'E'**liminate our **'F'**ears, *'Grief'* becomes the only logical emotion and assumed antidote for us to informally in an unconscious, yet conscious manner surrender to.

What would life look and feel like if humanity at an early stage understood the scientific meanings of numbers?

What would happen if every time something happened in our lives, instead of instinctively reacting to any disturbing stimuli, if we would instinctively calculate the numbers and their significance readily apparent in any given situation to logically determine what our reactions should be?

What would happen to our fears about **Death, Dying,** and **Grief**, if we all had an understanding of the significance of numbers and how to calculate them?

I propose that with this esoteric insight into "GRIEF" and the scientific significance relating to understanding numbers and letters, we can form definite emotional resolutions about death, dying, anger, denial, depression, bargaining, and acceptance of these seemingly insurmountable illnesses with greater opportunities to overcome all fear-based emotions.

Growth is an extension of Grief and challenges us to realize that no matter what happens, *"Life is still worth Living!"*

—NET-HETEP TA'NESERT

CONTENTS

CHAPTER ONE

Celebrate Progress, Life, Fearlessly!

Portion of the Original Twins "0/O": Original Level of Our Inner Support Systems

Grief empowers our ability to Grow.
It is the original microcosmic twin a reflection of the above.
An agreement we all made to come to earth.
In order to reach transformation's summit, we must pass through the gates of 'Grief'.
Focus tenaciously on the 'O' within Grow, the microcosmic twin of the macrocosmic womb known as Zero.
Can we not see that there are other similarities in the letters G/R doing their best to get our attention?
O heavenly celestial wombs giving birth to the first minor 9 pOtent possibilities,
teach us to understand the languages of your mysterious children who are
The exoteric keepers who will not speak until humanity is ready to understand their esoteric significance.
Acting as a combination of numerical reasons, manifesting as cycles for everything happening in our lives as we strive to reach upward to transformation's
summit in order to become one with you again.

Atyeb Ba Atum Re

The Waters above the Waters

Our journey inward and upward began long before our terrestrial conception. We must remember that all things have an origin and originate infused with dualistic personalities within the first oldest twin, the macrocosmic digit '0'. The first evidence of our inner support systems with particular qualities such as fortitude, articulation, awareness of subtleties and astute inner perceptions began on this level. The digit '0' is respected universally as the great womb of the "Everything and Nothing whose sum total equals 'infinity' (aka the Source), recognized as the entry way for all other numbers. Acting as a Super Parent, it officially in-fuses each number with a specific vibration designated to teach continual lessons of growth, cyclically. Here is where our quest to redefine grief must begin. To do this and experience measura-ble results requires full participation on the part of those burdened with the beastly natures of grief. To experience a breakthrough involving the messages speaking to us from each companion of grief such as: Anger, Denial, Depression, Bar-gaining, and Acceptance, each individual must be willing to discover the significant meanings of letters and their association with the esoteric language of numbers.

Grief bombards our astute inner support systems with traumatic incidents such as death, and detachment through loss of our loved ones, health, homes, failed relationships, poverty, wars, and all

10

other fear causing events. The mental disorders that we develop from our inner senses constant saturation of foreboding pessimistic events transforms our original level positive qualities into adverse qualities of anger, denial, guilt, and bargaining. These first four debilitating qualities are the champions of transformation.

Why?

Systematically, they abruptly create pivotal spirals of confusion, forcing us to seek out information that will logically answer our questions. Information is extremely crucial at this point. Our hearts and minds spiral outward erratically into numerous directions, demanding explanations and reasons for these atrocious circumstances happening in our lives. Therefore, 'Grief', which is the sum total of these individual qualities challenges us to go within ourselves to seek out the answers, metaphorically symbolizing returning to the 'Great Womb, the digit 0" where everything first began. Willingly, we will spiral upward again using our inner support systems positive qualities, transformed into both subconscious and conscious levels of spiritual and physical 'perceptions of acceptance'. This level of growth causes us to submit eventually to a reality of changing our definitions and perceptions of the appearances of sudden traumatic situations, only if we can graduate from the first four debilitating adverse qualities within the hideous realms of 'Grief'.

It is not a coincidence that the microcosmic twin, the letter 'O' is in the numerical column of the exoteric six, esoterically. Just as there are dual connotations of numbers, the same applies to information tailored for the public, termed as being exoteric. This level of information wears the mask of concealment. It conceals the necessary information needed to address and provide real reasons pertaining to traumatic situations, which would de-stress the public, and potentially assist with living healthier lives. Whereas, information tailored for private, smaller groups of people provides greater insights into everyday affairs enabling them to react differently to traumatizing events is termed as being esoteric, which enables this group to live healthier, minimally stress-free lives.

1	2	3	4	5	6	7	8	9
A	B	C	D	E	F	G	H	I
J	K	L	M	N	O	P	Q	R
S	T	U	V	W	X	Y	Z	

The most ancient civilizations originating around Africa's Nile Valley taught other ancient civilizations before the emergence of Europe, the significant language of numbers astronomically, and astrologically, as well as other life yielding advantages. (Branch-New York Times, 1990)

Therefore, on an exoteric level the numeric personalities of the number six is associated with the adverse qualities of the letter 'O', while on an esoteric level there exists the positive qualities of the letter 'O'. One of the very important aspects of this 'O' is that it is a vowel whose esoteric meaning has notable qualities tied to justice and balance. Astronomically, it is associated with the planet Saturn who astrologically is said to be the disciplinarian of our planet. Justice and Balance is the obscure message of Saturn. Additionally, it is also associated with the element of water, which provides ample energetic vibrations infused with heightened sensitivities for spiritual judgment. It carries the responsibility of being able to understand on any level the legalities of cause and effect-the ideal versus reality. Vowels provide immaterial substances with numerous platforms to become materialized forms once orally spoken.

Positive and Adverse Personalities of the O

sympathetic	sensitive to criticism
generous	lack of will
intuitive	dogmatic
strong sense of justice	critical
organized	fear of failure
faithful	suppressed emotions
tenacious	mournful

Religions purposefully have imprisoned the psyche of the masses with their misleading interpretations of the adverse qualities of

the number 6 without revealing the positive numerical personalities of the number 6 as well. Here is a small list of some of the
favorable numerical personalities of the number 6:

- unconditional love
- harmony/balance
- empathetic
- home/family
- self-sacrificing
- willing to compromise
- humanitarianism
- nurturing
- caring
- visionary
- honesty/integrity
- just and justice

Over extended periods with the constant bombardment of particular stimuli, not only is our psyche affected, our genetic coding
becomes infected with these one-sided interpretations. Notice
that the consonant 'F' (Fear) also occupies the numeric personality of the number 6. The consonant 'F' in cabalistic sciences is
exalted with the spirited qualities of achieving harmony through
constructive expression balanced with the usage of one's will, and
intellect. However, things must be viewed differently. It can also

give life to an inward sense of cheerfulness to be used for one's physical life. Pessimism and incorrect idealism must be avoided. It is easy to understand how if this information was taught to humanity early during its adolescent stages, all fear based related words containing the consonant 'F' would not be so frightening to our psyche. Alternatively, humanity would naturally examine its own emotions with confidence when caught off guard by life's random, and oftentimes shocking events.

Within various fields of science, numbers are referred to as, 'ethers'. These pleasant smelling and colorless liquids are assigned to particular degrees (numbers) of being volatile or highly flammable. Science understands that when they are experimenting with various combinations of these ethers, the combinations must be compatible. Ethers are very unpredictable, which explains their connection with our emotions. Our bodies are delicate compositions of these unpredictable ethers, which is why in the medical field patient charts exist. Our charts are nothing but various combinations of numbers (ethers). Traumatic experiences, instantly causes our delicate ethers to go into chaotic states of becoming explosives; hence, the old cliché, "Walking time bombs."

When those who work in the medical field check out our vital signs, what exactly are they checking? What we think, eat, and drink also can cause these numerical combinations within our bodies to fluctuate wildly. When this happens, all of the various systems designed to keep us functioning properly inward sends numerical messages chemically that those trained in the medical field are able to read.

What we must remember foremost above All things is that All things have both a non-physical and physical representation. However, when forced to confront grief's adverse qualities, we immediately are prone to forget about the existence of opposites or duality because of our relentless attachments to materialized forms. The beautiful result is having a small portion of under-standing the dualistic natures of the original twins "0/O" along with tools provided to each of us through our inner support systems is in place for a resolved demeanor or to accept these uncomfortable lessons of transformation and from them be inspired to "Grow".

CHAPTER TWO

Trust and Grow. Let's Go!

1	2	3	4	5	6	7	8	9
A	B	C	D	E	F	G	H	I
J	K	L	M	N	O	P	Q	R
S	T	U	V	W	X	Y	Z	

Making Friends with Grief and its Best Friends

"They Want to Talk to Us"

Already, I can hear your thoughts. Maybe you just sat there and said it aloud.

"Making friends with grief and its best friend's they want to talk to us?"

"Who in their right minds would want to do that?"

Grief and its recognized best friends such as Anger, Denial, Depression, Fear and its other best friend, "Acceptance" are words that have been used to trigger imbalances within our logical and emotional minds (conscious and subconscious). Their vibrations are so strong that they infect our mental and physical immune systems.

However, they really do not mean to. What they really want is for us to learn how to understand them and their messages. To do that, we must use numerology.

Let us start with the ringleader, 'Grief'.

On a piece of paper write the word 'grief' down and then underneath each letter write the numbers that you see above.

G R I E F

7 9 9 5 6

Now add them up.

G R I E F

7+ 9+ 9 +5 + 6= 36= 3+ 6= 9

Wow!

"New Beginnings Increases Humanity's Chances to Experience Universal Love"

Who would have ever imagined that fearsome word, "GRIEF" is the gateway to new beginnings for those of us who are living *survivors* after our loved ones transition, and or after a divorce, a hurtful relationship ended, loss of a job, health, etc?

Okay, now let us become friends with 'grief' by having an intimate conversation with its individual numerical messages.

G R I E F

$7 + 9 + 9 + 5 + 6 = 36 = 3 + 6 = 9$

Amazing!

"New Beginnings Increases Humanity's Chances to

Experience Universal Love"

Yes! *Collective Consciousness* is the positive message that the number 7 is singing about at the beginning of this subliminally, mentally fearful word. It is encouraging US to use all of OUR faith and spirituality to endure this difficult moment only for a little while.

What is happening?

19

Even with all of the emotional questioning we do during these difficult moments, what is truthfully going on ultimately is that "GROWTH" is challenging us to experience a ***spiritual awakening***.

The number 7, petitions us to feel the awesome *awareness* waiting in this moment full of limitless possibilities for us to utilize the wisdom _WE_ have accumulated to rise above all challenges.

Some of the other wonderful conversations we can have with this number while we are grieving are considering that it is also telling us to *look deep within ourselves*. In addition, we must leave room in our grieving space to take the time to understand others through *demonstrating thoughtfulness* while displaying we have the "***ability to bear hardships***". The assisting tools offered to us through the language of the number 7 are:

- *inner-wisdom*
- *spiritual acceptance*
- *development of your endurance*
- *Perseverance through the persistence of purpose to be at peace.*

It wants us to remain *poised* while *controlling our emotions and feelings* during this challenging moment.

Meanwhile, society naturally embraces the number 7s lower vibrations of *depression, inactivity*, and becoming *anti-social* while going through this challenging moment after the transitioning of a loved one or loss of a job, having to end a hurtful relationship, and or some other traumatizing experience. We tend to yield to lengthy periods being *resentful* and *showing resentment* to others around us or just *blame life* for our ills during these moments. The lower vibrations of the number 7 oftentimes sends us to darkened places causing us to go into a *phase of silence*, or demonstrating the *inability to share* our emotions. We may become *stagnant, lacking the ability to be persistent* about rediscovering our joy for wanting to continue living. Furthermore, as we become more and more *pessimistic* towards life and our immediate environments, we could in addition to everything else stemming from the lower vibrations of the number 7; we could lean towards being *argumentative*.

When we know how to do the math that, everyone hints at as knowing that the statement is a mind teaser towards society, which does not know how to do the real math. Numbers talk!

There are two major players back to back in the word 'gRIef. Their numerical presence is that powerful consciousness number 9^2 (If I be lifted up, I will draw all to me-there are two number 9s which indicates a greater electromagnetism to its individual value).

If we were to multiply the 9 twice= 81= 8+1= 9, the sum total of the secret weapon hiding with 'grief' that doubles its electro-negative effects within our mental and physical selves are the numbers 8 and 1. In addition to that, its sum total is another hidden (unseen) 9 vibration. Therefore, in actuality we have 9^3. Let's see if that will change the equation from its current sum total.

G R I E F

$7+9+9^3+5+6=45=4+5=9$

PREVIOUS SUM TOTAL

Without the addition of the hidden value was

$36=3+6=9$

Either way we sum it up, it is still

A 9!

PooOW! BaaAM!

DROP THA MIC!

Life is a mystical journey...

You're not alone

CHAPTER THREE

At the End Is A New Beginning Intensified!

"New Beginnings Increases Humanity's Chances to

Experience Universal Love"

CHOOSE WISELY

What that means is the longer you grieve, the greater the chances are for you to experience the extreme levels of *remorse, anger, sorrowfulness, depression, suicidal thoughts*, or seek out ways to escape the challenge of **'ACCEPTANCE'**. Usually this will mean experimenting with various forms of *addictive substances*.

At the other end of the pole, once we are able to process our pain, a GREAT HEALING AWAITS US ALL. We can choose joy, laughter, peace, wisdom from the experience and so much more-Life more abundantly.

Why?

The number 9s message is at the end is a new beginning. Life will start over because it's cyclic. It also speaks of integrity, and wisdom.

UNIVERSAL LOVE to the THIRD POWER awaits us when we make friends with "GRIEF and all other fear-based emotions".

The other famously phenomenal headliners are:

- Faith
- Karma
- Spiritual Enlightenment
- Spiritual Awakening
- Humanitarianism
- Philanthropist
- Soul Mission
- Soul Purpose
- Generosity
- Higher Perspective
- Inner Strength
- Strength of Character
- Wisdom
- Non-Conformity
- Forgiveness
- Compassion
- Empathy/Sympathy

- In addition, so much more on a positive vibe to the third power or three-fold!

The next grand conversationalist vibing along with the others in this world renowned, frightening gang is the number '5'. The heart purifying clout it possesses are actually refreshing qualities and just what our spiritual hearts are asking for in efforts to elevate us to the next level of "GROWTH".

Remember, we are all on an earthly journey with a direction in mind. The direction acts as a crescendo to our final destination.

The joyful noise (lol) that '5' is making goes by the diverse sounds heard within ***"LIFE LESSONS of LEARNED EXPERIENCES"***. The reasons why the sounds are so diverse are that everyone is seeking to customize what influences the idiosyncrasies of their personal exemptions. Life overstands our inability to respond to the higher esoteric conversations speaking within the '5' because generations keep on passing without mainstream society having these sciences introduced publically into its educational systems. Therefore, this form of information sounds foreign-SOUNDS LIKE NOISE.

Quite naturally, we continue the cycle of fearing 'grief' and reacting inappropriately. We keep conforming to acting out impetuously, reckless, imprudent, and thoughtless. The next notable behavior and ***expected*** behavior we exhibit are moments of being unreliable, inconsistent, and fearful of commitment. In those, ground '0' moments, our hearts and minds, besieged with psychotic thoughts, screaming demands at us to change our rigid thoughts, actions, and stagnant routines. All chaotic experiences are strategies from life's lessons "Growth Department". Their purposes are tailored to bring discord and turmoil into our 'environ-mental states of being. We experience stages of restlessness, psychologically as well as biologically. Ingeniously updated it has proven to be massively effective for centuries.

The Age of Information is an opportunity for humanity to demonstrate its courage to take unconventional steps towards proclaiming its:

- Adaptability
- Versatility
- Individualism
- Resourcefulness
- Motivation
- Progress
- Adventure
- Companionability
- Sociability
- Health and Healing
- Pleasure loving
- Being Opportunistic

- Kindness, sympathy and understanding
- Vivacious
- Magnetic
- Curiosity
- Visionaries
- Intelligently making decisions
- Excited about the limitless choices living provides us

Wow, that is a grand conversation indeed, especially when we have received the esoteric memo about who just showed up in 'Growth's Department' as a tumultuous situation.

The next motivational speaker numerically has celebrity status and is sought after by everyone. It is none other, than everyone's favorite, surprise!-it is the number '6' whose vibrations and frequencies reign supreme as *"UNCONDITIONAL LOVE"*. Who would have thought that such a powerful and world-renowned frequency is a nurturing part of our grieving processes? Now, with this in mind, surely we all should be eager to know the other redeeming attributes of this motivational speaker. As a motivational speaker who is longing for your attention while you are grieving is saying, "Hey, let's talk. I can help you through this.

My qualifications consist of:

- Tranquility
- Peace

- Unity
- Understanding
- Home and Family
- Nurturing
- Self-Sacrifice
- Service to Others
- Empathy and Sympathy
- Parenthood
- Selflessness and Responsibility
- Care
- Honesty and Integrity
- Healing
- Burden bearing
- Humanitarianism
- Possessing the ability to Compromise
- Protection
- Just and Justice
- Seeing Clearly
- Grace and Dignity
- Reliable
- Provider
- Idealistic
- Faithfulness
- Honor and Honesty . . ."

All of these conversationalists numerically have a down side to them. Life's lessons "Growth Department" shows compassion towards the human experience by making provisions for us to go through a time of being weak-willed, restless while showing moments of selfishness. It creates the occasions for us to have a superiority complex and think that it is okay to be impractical, shallow, passive, and easily stressed.

Numerically, this becomes more and more exciting because when we calculate the various, profoundly revealing, types of conversations that we have had so far with the word 'Grief', and its best friends, making friends with them is becoming easier. We have two different ways to reach a final conclusion to this word that causes everyone to be filled with fear when and wherever we have to encounter its presence in our lives for various inescapable reasons. Let's look back at its first sum total before considering the second one. Again, we must refresh our memories with how we got the numbers by reconstructing our letter and number, de-ciphering chart.

1	2	3	4	5	6	7	8	9
A	B	C	D	E	F	G	H	I
J	K	L	M	N	O	P	Q	R
S	T	U	V	W	X	Y	Z	

G R I E F

7+9+9+5+6 =36=3+6=9 (1st consideration)

Before we can finalize the 1st consideration, a new conversation-alist is introduced in life's lessons 'Growth Department Representatives' within its client 'Grief', whom we are learning can be something that we can make friends with along with its best friends, who want to make friends with us as well. We are glad to introduce to our conscious mind and heart the soulful number, '3'.

Making friends with this number is easy because most of our minds that are religious immediately associate the number '3' with the triune Godhead. There are many happy mental associa-tions connected to this number. Below are just a few examples.

- Three Wise Men
- Three Pyramids of Giza
- Three Little Pigs
- Goldilocks and the Three Bears

There is no way any of us would suspect this wonderful number would even want to be one of grief's best friends, numerically. Right? What could it possibly have to say to us? It's like finding out that one of your best friends is hanging out with a bad group of people or a person.

Well, let's just see what it has to say for itself and why it's one of grief's best friends.

Here are the loyal, reliable, reverberating, and undulating characteristics of the number 3 that you have come to love.

- Optimism
- Joy
- Compassion
- Inspiration
- Creativity
- Humor
- Good Taste
- Spontaneity
- Courageous
- Adventurous
- Encouraging
- Passionate
- Enthusiastic
- Intuitive
- Non-Confrontational
- Interested in Growth and Expansion
- Broad-minded
- Artistic
- Youthfulness
- Talented and has skills

- Witty, loves fun and pleasure
- Imaginative
- Intelligence
- Speech and Communication-Wow!

The number '3' is believed to also resonate with the 'Ascended Masters' who are interested in helping us to concentrate on the divine spark of peace, clarity and love residing deep within us. All we need to do is ask for their help.

When we are grieving, we forget to all of the joyous and divine assistance available to us pulsating from this number. Therefore, if we are going to experience its low vibrations of having *mood swings, bouts of depression, indifference* and a *lack of stamina* along with the *inability to focus*, our visitation on its lower vibrations should not be long. We have so much more to reach inward to and make grief and its best friends our greatest allies when having to detach from anything. What do you think?

There are two major players back to back in the word 'gRIef. Their numerical presence is that powerful consciousness number 9^2 (If I be lifted up, I will draw all to me-there are two number 9s which indicates a greater electromagnetism to its individual value).

If we were to multiply the 9 twice= 81= 8+1= 9, the sum total of the secret weapon hiding with 'grief' that doubles its electro-negative effects within our mental and physical selves are the numbers 8 and 1. In addition to that, its sum total is another hidden (unseen) 9 vibration. Therefore, in actuality we have 9^3. Let's see if that will change the equation from its current sum total.

GRIEF

$7+9+9^3+5+6=45=4+5=9$ (2nd consideration)

There are two other factors living within the 2nd consideration. One is the number 9s electromagnetism increases three-fold, which means it's like upgrading to a super size meal, and a premium deal associated with its positive characteristics. Secondly, a new best friend wants to talk to us and it's the practical number '4'. To convince us that we should make it our best friend as well are these features:

- Trust and Trust-worthiness
- Organization and Exactitude
- Patience
- Loyalty
- High morals
- Conscientiousness
- Realistic Values

- Dependability
- Stability
- Discipline
- Determination
- Service
- Devotion
- Progress and Development
- Management skills
- Builds solid foundations
- Methodical
- Resonates with the Archangels-unbelievable

Its low vibrations are so few that we could easily avoid them if we know about '4s' finer qualifications as a best friend. They will show up in our moods as wanting to be lazy, have a lack of conviction for handling our responsibilities, along with an inability to adapt to change.

Before discovering how we're going to become even greater best friends to the word "Grief", we will summarize this portion by understanding the culminating message of grief is one of experiencing a "SPIRITUAL AWAKENING with a NEW BEGINNING".

This is how we do the *'Math'* that leads to profound growth, spiritually and mentally awakening us all to experience new beginnings in life after surviving any type of loss.

CHAPTER FOUR

Do the Math. It's Fun!

Intimate Messages from each letter in the word GRIEF

The amazing thing about all of this is that if we apply these sciences, they truly have the potential to change our reactions when we encounter unexpected turmoil and detachment from things that we have grown accustomed too.

Imagine this with me for a few moments… close your eyes and feel the love of our inner selves reacting from passionate, soul stirring frequencies and vibrations of supreme understanding within any given encounter of misfortune, trauma and any chaotic situation that becomes a triumphant testimony of thankfulness as a living magnificent creation from supreme love. While experiencing these moments of what has traditionally performed as sorrowful, mournful and overwhelmingly sad moments, we would instead truly introduce a soothing level of pure intimacy of understanding what is happening, so that our loved ones could really transition to heaven in blissful waves of peace, and tranquility.

Let's journey now together, hand in hand with open minds into a wonderful new age of discovering the esoteric (real) meanings of letters. They too seek to become our best friends and loving allies to new depths of expansion for our souls. All we need to do is fine tune our inner ears to their uniquely, soothing, uplifting nurturing messages being conveyed to us if we would just stop and listening to them. Grief and all of its best friends want to become a soulful, transformational, universal rhythm and an epoch song.

Front and Center, immediately taking the leadership role in the terrifying, clinically studied word-Grief-respectfully is the consonant 'G'. Control your emotions. (York) Don't back away from taking this breath and taking a second to discover the wonderful, esoteric con-versations that the entire world should be sharing with each other each time we find ourselves facing moments causing us to grieve about various things.

Its leading conversation first speaks to us about "Endowments of Conviction and Acumen". Along with it are its companion colors, 'deep blue, and silvery blue'. Endowments of Conviction and Acumen addresses what qualities and abilities we all possess inwardly, coupled with a firm belief, opinion, stance and or position about something. Acumen simply speaks about being able to make quick decisions, clever, sharp-witted, and smart within a certain domain. Life is definitely a certain domain, challenging us daily to experience "Growth".

36

In addition to that, the consonant *'G'* is associated with *"MOON"*. We all know that the moon controls the ebb and flows of the emotional oceans of life. No, wonder, this explains why we are so deeply impacted emotionally when we are grieving. The second and most valuable conversation that the consonant 'G' discusses is how it is actually enabling us to utilize our spiritual gifts from previous lives, to facilitate the necessary understanding and acceptance of the current moment-AND MOVE FORWARD. It speaks about "Perseverance, Patience, and Memory".

When we are grieving, the consonant 'G' is pleading with us to prepare ourselves to transmute our sorrows into 'Celebrating Garments of Spiritual Confidence'. We must learn to put our spiritual convictions into action. Our greatest tasks that this consonant calls forth are for us to conquer sarcasm, anger, depression, and bitterness. It blows a trumpet sounding out our abilities to balance peace and discord within our personal being for our sake, as well as for other surviving loved ones. We can utilize this awareness in every area of our lives.

Wouldn't you agree?

We can go even further by examining the consonant 'Gs' symbolic character, exoterically (outer structure hiding its esoteric-real-nature) conveying nonverbal information. It is of monumental priority that we approach this part of our awakening from a higher state of consciousness. We are entering into the realm of the "Most Holy of Holies-Divine Intercourse" and its most intimate alchemical expressions of divine creation in the forms of pictographs (Spiritual Letters Esoterically used as Mundane Letters Exoterically).

$$***C -***G***$$

Obviously, we have an open crescent with a horizontal traversing dash. What we're looking at is the symbol for divine intercourse in the pre-stages of cosmic copulation. Once it penetrates, the lower lip of the open crescent who willfully awaits the passing through of the horizontal traversing dash it appears to form the consonant 'G'. Divine copulation is taking place, seeding the open crescent with powerful new expressions of both spiritual, and physical transmutations. Our abilities to change (transmute) our traumatic experiences into learned outwardly expressions of recognized paths of knowing that "Life is Still Worth Living-No Matter What", can be compared allegorically with knowing what it is like being pregnant. There is the joy of intimately experiencing procreation and then there is the reality of undetermined grieving time acting like the birthing pangs. However, when we endure these faith crippling situations, like proud parents when we emerge from 'grief's gloomy shadows', we hold in our arms, loving testaments of our convictions to rise above any threatening-knock down blows from life. Transmutation can only take place when we fully participate in these events. Our cellular framework on an alchemical level acts as the ovum, while our higher mind turns into fertilizing creative sparks exploding into spiritual ecstasy, helping us to intimately design our own "Ark of Agreements, Divine Chalices, and Holy of Holies."

Finally, the consonant 'G' rightfully stands, profoundly at the forefront of the word 'Grief' declaring that it is there manifesting itself invisibly as pain, suffering and sorrow as an intimate witness and silent watcher, recording our behavior while we're experiencing another growth spurt for life's lessons archives. It also simultaneously kneels in prayer waiting for us to rise above the current sorrowful situations causing us to misunderstand its intimate messages. During those antagonizing, heart wrenching moments that feel like an eternity of pain, this consonant is beckoning us to embrace the spiritual dynamism in our possession to generate *"HAPPINESS, PEACE,* and welcome the *STRENGTH IN COMFORTS EMBRACE* to effectively create new life experiences".

The consonant 'G's' next personal and bosom confidant is the "Fiery Letter of Love, Wisdom and Freedom-blazing in colors of amber, and oranges astrologically associated with the Majestic *Sun*, is the consonant *"R"*. This may sound unbelievable because of its grime association with the word 'grief' however; its strongest message to us is one of 'inspiration to love wisely and freely'.

39

Latent in each of us is a unique force customized to allow individualized expressions of our intense experiences with physical life. Fire in this sense, represents will power, determination, tenacity and drive to walk through each challenging fires of constant growth and change.

The degree of difficulty lies in the amount of "PERPETUAL EFFORT and APPLICATION" of the wisdom, you have freely acquired while traveling through, up and over the various terrains of spiritual, mental and physical journeys of 'Transformation'.

Just like the consonant 'G', we will dissect this glyph as well. From this moment forward let us all try to develop the mindset to really see the bigger pictures expressed in our pictorial alphabets.

Look at the geometric shapes connected in the 'R' closely.

*** ⭕ ***❘ ***＼ = ℞

Can you see three different shapes (geometric conversations) that come together to create this powerful structure of Love?

1. Upper Circle symbolizing the spiritual abode that nourishes us all universally with, _knowledge_ of _supreme love_, experiences that produce _wisdom._

2. Vertical Line (s) in most artistic principles of design represents direction, and action. In this experience, it is accessing the spiritual wisdom of the above and drawing

it down into our physical experiences. Remember this is a continual pipeline to inexhaustible sources of inspiration, reminding us of our constant connection to and with Supreme Love.

3. Lastly, there is the 'Diagonal Line', extending itself from the 'Upper Circle'. Another activating line on the physical level signaling us to be more conscious as we intuitively utilize the strength available to us constantly and spiritually, whether we acknowledge it or not. Notice that the diagonal line draws us in closer to experience events that will require greater activation of our spiritual fortitude in order to experience sublime transformational moments meant to cause us to grow.

When we try to restrict experiencing the necessary lessons meant to further our knowledge and wisdom needed to help us understand these traumatic encounters, we are aiding the forces of strife, stress, and depression to gain frightening foot holes in our lives. In turn, this creates our inability to utilize the strength found in love to overcome this ground zero leveling emotional experiences in our lives.

If we let our lives symbolize the sun, during those heartbreaking moments, we can help, but to realize that as the sun continues to rise and shine-SO MUST WE.

The sun shines before storms, after storms and sometimes while it is storming. How does it manage that? It is a meteorological phenomenon known as a "Sun Shower". Rain falls while the sun is shining accompanied by strong winds from a rainstorm that is actually happening somewhere else. These strong winds have the ability to blow the airborne raindrops into places where rain clouds are not in that area. Even the angle of the sun when a storm is passing by can cause that area to experience a sun shower. Meteorologically, if the angle of the sun is low enough it will cause the appearance of a 'rainbow'. Imagine that!

While the storms of life is raging, with the right mental attitude we can see our lives at that very challenging moment as a "Sun Shower" and our intense will to push forward creating a life of joy, happiness, peace and serenity takes on the transformation of becoming "RAINBOWS".

Generosity is also associated with this fiery glyph of love, wisdom, and freedom. The more we experience growth from these life-changing circumstances, the more we come to understand that we have much to offer to ourselves, and those in our immediate environment. The more we grow, the more we can give back to the reservoirs of life, which if we transform our tragedies into useful life changing solutions for others will eventually become like healing 'sun showers', freely reminding us at all times that –*Life is still worth living.*

Another challenging, yet intimate message this shape shifter makes us aware of is our attachment to what makes us feel secure. It causes us to examine our security issues with life. After careful and close examine of the materialistic attachments that we've bonded with, when they have been altered through loss of any kind, the glyph 'R' still strongly speaks to us about remembering that we have the ability to manifest security on any level for ourselves using the 'Spiritual Fires of love, wisdom and freedom'.

Finally, this glyph of fiery spiritual love, wisdom and freedom, asks three things of us that will completely activate its intimate message within us.

We must develop:

1. Humility
2. Gratitude
3. Devotion

The development of these three things ensures that we will always be able to see both sides of an issue. Willingly, our actions inspire others to pursue the right course of action freely for themselves, utilizing their own inner knowing of self-worth guided by higher perceptions of love, exercised through the fiery spiritual wisdom gained from their own experiences.

Be Inspirational To Others

Intimate Messages from each Letter

Meet the Secret Weapons in All Languages

"THE VOWELS"

It is no secret that vowels are the power in every language. The esoteric frequencies latent within consonants need vowels to activate them. Vowels are cardinal points and related to archangels, elements, astrological signs, and nature beings. Therefore, the intimate messages spoken from the vowels cloaked throughout languages fuel the emotions that we connect with in words. They have the abilities to strike directly at our hearts. They are forces that activate the various emotions we experience when others push our buttons depending on their tones when they speak certain words.

In Ancient Egypt, the four sons of Horus represented not only the internal organs; they also represented the four main cardinal points.

Emhotep.net

Duamutef	**Qebehsenuef**	**Hapi**	**Imseti**
of the East	of the West	of the North	of the South
Guardian of the	Guardian of the	Guardian of the	Guardian of the
Stomach	**Intestines**	**Lungs**	**Liver**

Vowels

I [S]   **U [N]**   **O [W]**   **E [E]**

In the beginning was the creation WORD

The Egyptian Krast (Christ) is Osiris

A= Ether (Androgynous)

All four Cardinal Directions

All Four Nature Beings

The heart stays with the body because it is believed to house the soul.

Redefine Your Fears and Rejoice!

Michael   Raphael   Gabriel   Uriel

ATUN-RE   *AMUN-RE*   *ANUN-RE*   *ATUM-RE*

The suns of RE borrowed by the Greeks from the Egyptian Mysteries. RE's small name in the Egyptian Mysteries is Elul, which forms the last part "EL" on the end of each name of the Angels in the Bible.

In the Western Culture, the vowels and their associated arche-

types and astrological associations are as follows:

Vowel	Element	Direction	Archangel	Nature Beings
A	ETHER	ALL FOUR	CHRIST	ALL FOUR
E	AIR	EAST	RAPHAEL	SYLPHS
I	FIRE	SOUTH	MICHAEL	SALAMAN-DERS
O	WATER	WEST	GABRIEL	UNDINES
U	EARTH	NORTH	AURIEL	GNOMES

47

Astrological/Vowel/Elemental Personality

Astrological	Vowel	Elemental Personality
Ether is highest spiritual material that permeates through all elements and substances	A	Ambition, acumen, adaptability, creative, focused, honest, goal oriented, emotionally sensitive, dis-organized, possessive, self-indulgent, lack of will determination
Gemini/Libra/Aquarius	E	Innovative, intellectual, perspicacious, agile, observant, collaborative, humanitarian, aloof, deceptive, skittish, careless
Aries/Leo/Sagittarius	I	Bravery, audacious, idealistic, supportive, prolific interpretation, capable, energetic, commanding, extremist, hedonistic, strict
Cancer/Scorpio/Pisces	O	Balance, competent, intuitive, Loves the Arts, sociable, kind, aloof, fearful, dogmatic, lacks determination, moody, overly exaggerates
Taurus/Virgo/Capricorn	U	Provider, established, time perceptive, highly intuitive, progressive, gentle, selfish, unsympathetic, secretive, narrow-minded, arrogant

The other amazingly wonderful areas that vowels affect are our inner support energy systems in our bodies, also known chakra centers. If you are new to this term, its origin is 'Sanskrit', which means wheel or cycle. In Tanzania, Central Africa there is a mountain that is sacred to that region known as Mount Meru. The journey from the bottom to the top represents the progressions and pathways of life. Therefore, as one travels from the bottom of Mount Meru to the top, our energy flows from the 'Root chakra to the Crown chakra throughout our bodies in a circle, and cycle like fashion.

Furthermore, in both ancient Egyptian and Indian traditions Mount Meru is present, which means the Tantra System since the beginning of human life on this planet is commonly known to both cultures. The sacred sciences taught in this system include the chakras, kundalini, Hatha yoga, Astronomy (Aset-Egyptian Goddess) and Astrology (same Egyptian Goddess). Both of these Sciences are Feminine. Re-member, the Dravidian people are descendants of Ethiopia and the majority of the Indian yoga teachings we are learning today have their origins in Africa.

More importantly, is the fact that these inner support energy systems in our bodies are connected to the vowels. What this means is that our energy centers are activated, constantly as we think, speak, read and write. We are made to feel certain emotions even when we hear and speak to each other.

However, once you the reader (s) have awareness of the positive and negative frequencies of our alphabet and numbers, after read-ing the information in this book, willingly facing daily events after each initial shock will slowly become easier.

Knowing this information is not meant to numb or desensitize us. It is meant to help us to began to really use our human senses in a more rational, logical and practical manner, which enables us to recover from traumatic experiences faster with peace of mind. The healing processes can take place easier when we have something that can spiritually, mentally and physically aide us in effectively evaluating,and processing our human emo-tions.

What are words? What are Emotions? What are Hu-man Emotions?

Why do they control how we Think?

Human Emotions

Grief grief *Grief* Grief **grief** Grief **Grief**
grief Γριεφ Grief **grief** Grief grief Grief
Decoded-Nothing to Fear

Let us recap what we have discovered so far before looking deeper into the intimate messages of the vowels, "E" and "I", af-ter which we will conclude the messages of "GRIEF", by examining the final consonant "F" before moving on to some of grief's other well known, and talked about little friends.

The consonant "G's" leading message speaks to us about "En-dowments of Conviction and Acumen".

We all possess different capabilities inwardly that we firmly be-lieve, know, and trust will assist us when we have to make sound and quick decisions in either a particular area, and or vari-ous areas as we encounter different living experiences. It also challenges us to transmute our personal knowledge of pain, suf-fering, and sorrows into useful tools of wisdom for ourselves, and humanity.

Meanwhile, the fiery spirited consonant "R" is all about devel-oping humility, devotion, and gratitude before its transforming

51

frequencies can fully be activated in each individual at any given moment. We all will need each one of the aforementioned activators, to correctly internalize, transmute, and the rightly utilize the spiritual transformers of "Love, Wisdom and Freedom".

Hmmm, the consonant 'R', increases the strength of any vowel that it is next to (gRIef). It actually expedites the chances for the hidden elemental personalities of that vowel to materialize its effects in the experience of the associated object, and or per-son (s). One of the other dynamic awareness of this consonant is, "security" is extremely essential. Usually, what challenges us the most when we receive traumatic news or sometime thereafter is our security in connection with things and or a person (s). However, the consonant 'R' is also a particular type of metaphysical superhero. It also enables us to achieve security on any level, so long as we have developed within our character the values of the three essential activators:

1. Humility
2. Devotion
3. And Gratitude

Further investigation will reveal when we do the math only on the consonants "G" and "R", it looks like this numerically and reveals a different type of duo message (remember we are exploring this information from an Esoteric perspective):

Refer to your Alpha-Numeric Chart from the previous pages

G=7   R=9

7+9=16=1+6=7

Here are a few of the numeric personalities of number 7, 9, 1, and 6:

7- Poise through life burdening moments is essential

- *inner-wisdom*
- *spiritual acceptance*
- *development of your endurance*
- *Perseverance through the persistence of purpose to be at peace*

9- Get ready for a new spiritual awakening because at the end is always a new beginning

- *spiritual enlightenment*
- *inner strength*
- *wisdom*
- *soul mission and purpose*
- *forgiveness*
- *compassion*

1- (New Insights) Perpetual movements in a forward direction ensures progress

- *positivity and optimism*
- *motivation*
- *strength through love*
- *tenacity*
- *inspiration and attainment*
- *happiness*
- *produce your own existence*

6- We can endure and be triumphant over all things utilizing "Unconditional Love"

- *Tranquility*
- *Peace*
- *Unity*
- *Understanding*
- *Home and Family*
- *Nurturing*
- *Self-Sacrifice*
- *Service to Others*
- *Empathy and Sympathy*

The sum total 16's message reminds us that thoughts are things.

We create our own realities with our thoughts. The reoccurring number is '7'. Keeping an open mind to new opportunities will help to build trust in one's self, while inspiring acceptance to 'GROW'.

Overall, immediately when we are ready to heal there are some very powerful blessings waiting to reveal themselves in our lives.

Claim those Blissings.
Say, Yes!

G-R-I-E-F

Getting Real Information Eliminates Fear

Intimate Messages from each letter in the word GRIEF

The final messenger in the word 'grief', before we meet the secret weapons in every language, is the auspicious agnate F.

It anchors and concretely establishes its presence to bring total balance to the scary word 'grief', which we are slowly revealing is not meant to be a frightening experience at all through the utilization of the dynamic forces of *"Attainment completed in Harmony"*. It is astrologically associated with the sign Taurus, ruled by the planet of love, Venus.

Self-regulation, self-regulation; Self-Regulation is the focal point of this beautiful glyph. Perpetual surveillance of our actions is highly required to safeguard us against behavioral patterns of inflexibility, and disgruntlement. The agnate 'F', incites us to view both and all sides to every situation so that we might learn how to remain optimistic, and open-minded to more advanced leverages.

Think Before You Act

Intimate Messages from each letter in the word GRIEF

Meet the Secret Weapons in All Languages

THE VOWELS

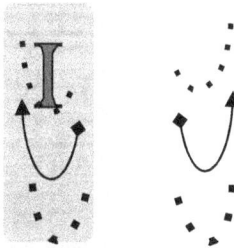

The ancient Egyptians were very cautious about excluding the vowels from their script within their sacred incantations.

Why?

They realized that these particular glyphs and their sounds were the abracadabra in all languages. We live in a time whereas what was once secret and sacred is now available for humanity to learn. The open awareness of this information remains sacred, when utilized to help humanity grow towards a greater understanding of its true connectivity with all things above as well as below. Information like this should be the focus of attention and taught in all spiritual systems, which would in turn enable its practitioners to operate their lives with greater overstanding, and acceptance of emotional changes as they occur in their lives every day.

Introducing, the first secret weapon in the word grief is the vowel "I". Remember, it is right next to the strongest activator the glyph 'R', which means all of the inherent electromagnetic personalities both positive and negative are ready to influence our reactions.

Surprisingly, the main ingredient of this secret weapon is 'Omnipresent Love'.

None of us would have ever imagined that such a powerful healing balm is one of the essential champions hidden within a heart wrenching word we all commonly share as human beings. Grief automatically is springing into spiritual medicinal action to start the healing processes needed to help sustain, nurture, soothe, and provide us with the inner strength needed to remember that life is still worth living.

True Story . . .

I can recall the very night that my mother transitioned. My doorbell rang in the middle of the night. I awakened from a strange dream, and in it, I was drowning. Immediately, when I saw one of my oldest brothers standing there, I felt like I was drowning in an immense tide of emotions. The fearful look on his face, confirmed the sudden shock, and reality that our mother had transitioned. The other horrible reality that his broken-hearted facial expression informed me of was that he was partly to blame for it. I let him inside and instinctively asked him, "What have you done to our mother?"

After he informed me of all occurrences, I drove us to the hospital. She was pronounced 'DOA'. A great many things grieved me during the whole transitioning processes. However, knowing this information helped me tremendously. I began looking for the treasures our mother left behind, which are always easily accessible to find in the memorable moments we shared. I knew she wanted all of us to be happy, and go on living no matter what-'Celebrating'.

Knowing that the vowel 'I' within the word grief meant the "omnipresent love" of the Divine was already present in that situation allowed me to heal and process that moment rapidly. I felt joy and happiness while others were weeping. I knew I would always miss her physical presence; however, I was able to *accept* her decision to transition at that moment in her life.

Here is a list of some of the other Omni-positive/negative personalities of the vowel 'I' to look for when you grieving, so you will learn to strive to balance your emotions with more of the positive personality traits of this vowel.

- Learn to see the law of source and consequences
- Integrate the Heart and Mind into healing expressions of compassion/healing
- Learn to control desires to take needless risks
- Strength bearing on all levels
- Attracts Love and Awareness through Comprehension
- Faithfulness and intuitive
- over-emotionalism
- greed
- over-indulgence
- hasty actions
- carelessness
- inertia
- alienation
- coldness
- possessiveness

- distrust

The overall message of this secret weapon in the word "Grief" is "Learn to transform pain, suffering, and sorrows utilizing the transmutation affluences of the "Omnipresent Love" factor

Let go! Let Love!

Nestled next to the fiery 'I' vowel is the airy "E" vowel, and together these two create some very powerful emotional reactions. What comes to your mind when 'fire and air' are present?

Wildfire? Things that are out of control? Destructive things?

Not only does the super vowel 'E' represent air, it also symbolizes the mind. In this case, to be more exact it symbolizes 'Perception and Universal Consciousness'. Perception and Universal Consciousness combined centers on how one arranges the exceptional thoughts conceived within one's subconscious (universal) mind that links exceptional thoughts or ideas with its normal consciousness. Harmony is the ultimate goal of this super vowel. Bringing things together to facilitate self- transformation by manifesting necessary situations for each person to encounter so that they may fulfill the vibratory mission of the super vowel 'E', this is about self-transformation by way of the vehicle known to humanity as

'Change'. Other concerned co-partners of 'perception' are 'trust and loyalty', along with the legitimate amalgamation of learned lessons from single, and or multiple life changing situations. Unifying all amalgamated parts with the correct perception after experiencing each unique situation is necessary in order to advance to the next level of one's transformational missions. The outcome is always one of assisting each person to live life more purposefully.

Here are some of the positive and negative qualities to measure your behavior by while experiencing situations during a grieving period.

Positive	**Negative**
Determination	Restless
Creative	Argumentative
Intuitive	Deceitful
Intellectual	Easily Irritated
Charismatic	Lacks Will Power
Esoterical	Dogmatic
Self- Mastery	Self-Righteous

We must remember to amalgamate the numerical personalities (I=9, E=5) with these vowels that are included with the overall message from the word 'Grief', which is "New Beginnings Increases Humanity's Chances to Experience Universal Love".

To increase our ability to nurture a healthy relationship with the word grief, let's examine the powerful numerical values of these super vowels from the perspective of two different mathematical equations.

Addition: I/E vowels

$9+5=14=1+4=5$

9= cyclic, integrity, wisdom, universal love, inner wisdom, soul's purpose, mission, higher perspective
5= relationships, freedom, discipline, life choices, non-attachments, courage, sympathy, empathy, release, surrender, visionary
1= creativity, confidence, adaptability, new beginnings, strength, self-reliance, love, inspiration, initiative, will power
4= foundations, methods, processes, procedures, practicality, service, devotion, trust, endurance

Multiplication: I/E vowels

$9 \times 5 = 45 = 4+5 = 9$

The experiment shows that even if the numerical personalities of the super vowels 'I/E' are intensified by magnifying their emotional vibrations felt using the multiplication process amalgamated with the mathematical function of Addition, the end result is still in harmony with Grief's overall message of ***"New Beginnings Increases Humanity's Chances to Experience Universal Love"***.

We will conclude with our findings with this final realization that GRIEF has a divine purpose. Its divine purpose does not intend to manifest experiences of Anger, Fear, Denial, Bargaining, Bitterness, and or Depression, as well as facing uncertainties about life through spiritual, mental, and physical Separation from the persons, places and things we've grown attached to while traveling through life towards our ultimate goal. Do not fear 'Death'. Our ultimate goal is to reach the peak of the summit of Transformation by way of mastering life's uniquely customized, and oftentimes chaotic, challenges of "GROWTH".

Divine love is the Goal

CHAPTER FIVE

!!ANGER!!

We all experience anger for one reason or another. It is normal or is it? Human reactions are great tools for assisting our souls to grow. It is a privilege to experience these emotions as we all seek ways to fulfill our soul's purpose and mission to aid in the further development of this planet and its inhabitants.

However, while we all incarnated and or reincarnated here to be Teachers, we have an even greater opportunity in front of us. The opportunity I am speaking of is learning the messages that come with these great lessons that we must also embrace-Emotionally. We can learn to overcome any fear-based emotion when we know how to decode its esoteric meaning. Each fear-based emotion has its own detrimental chemical that it releases into our biological bodies. When we have an understanding, we can lessen the long-term effects of these unbalancing chemicals, as soon as we move into a mode of acceptance.

Anger is not an emotion that we are born with. Anger is a learned emotion, according to Dr. Harry Mills (2005). Remember, we are all teachers and as infants, we learn from our immediate environment-FAMILY. When we become angry, our heart rate increases as well as we unconsciously began tensing the muscles in our bodies. Our bodies go through numerous reactions, which subsequently causes a release of 'adrenaline' into our bodies. Depending on the causes of anger, it can at times help us to defend ourselves-Fight or Flight syndrome.

These are just some of the exoteric effects of anger. If we want to overstand anger and not just manage it but also rather conquer it, then we must investigate its esoteric character.

1	2	3	4	5	6	7	8	9
A	B	C	D	E	F	G	H	I
J	K	L	M	N	O	P	Q	R
S	T	U	V	W	X	Y	Z	

$$A \quad N \quad G \quad E \quad R$$
$$1+5+7+5+9 = 27 = 2+7 = 9$$

Understanding our soul's mission and purpose through non-conformity

Well, well, well . . . don't you find that amazing? Grief and Anger have the same numerical personalities, yet their messages are different.

Understanding our soul's mission and purpose through non-conformity is 'anger's message'. The only difference it has from 'grief' is the letters involved and the numerical personalities. Therefore, it brings a different message by way of allowing us to view the phenomenon of universal love from a different angle relating to the circle of life . . . Non-Conformity.

Now that our format has revealed itself, we will start with letting the numerical personalities speak to us and then we will listen gratefully to the vowels and the consonants before moving on to make friends with the next socially frightening emotion . . . FEAR.

Fear will be your first workbook assignment that has included in the remaining parts of this book, along with other fear-based emotions for you to decode on your own. You will use the formula provided below that helped us to redefine 'Grief' and 'Anger'.

Numbers want to communicate with us. In actuality it is the intangible operating forces (elements, and or angelic) that are represented by numbers are earnestly yearning to communicate with US. They are used to build as well as destroy things, alchemically speaking. We know that accompanying them are tones. We certain words are spoken in a certain tone that too can infect the human psyche, which in turn affects the human body as well. This particular method is referred to as "pushing our human reactionary buttons".

We have already established our formula for solving and redefining these fear-based emotions.

1. *Calculate the sum total of their individual numerical personalities*

2. *Listen to each numerical personality's message*

3. *Have an open mind when making friends with the vowels involved because they are the secret and sacred powers in every word, in all languages-Elementally*

4. *The consonants are the friends to the vowels. They help the vowels to complete their missions as words that have power filled with divine meanings*

Research has shown that anger is a learned emotion, behaviorally through social conditioning. Therefore, non-conformity is vital. When we think about it, things that our environment has taught us to respond to in an upset manner is that really the best way to react? Do we conform because it is what we are taught is a natural reaction? What is healthy about learning how not to conform to what society dictates as being natural responses? Is it learning how to control our emotions? These questions open up an enormous portal to potentially new insights, into how consciousness is engineered by repetitive behavioral responses. Certain situations that seemingly are adverse to joy, peace, excellent health, and happiness when threatened expose us to reacting angrily.

1	2	3	4	5	6	7	8	9
A	B	C	D	E	F	G	H	I
J	K	L	M	N	O	P	Q	R
S	T	U	V	W	X	Y	Z	

A N G E R
1+5+7+5+9 = 27= 2+7=9

Understanding our soul's mission and purpose through non-conformity

Understanding our soul's mission and purpose through non-conformity

1= independence, uniqueness, motivation, striving forward, progress, ambition, will power, pioneering spirit, self-leadership, assertiveness, initiative, strength, self-reliance, organization, tenacity, love, inspiration, attunement, abilities to create one's own realities

Negative patterns= single-mindedness, intolerance, conceit, narrow-mindedness, weak will, dependence, passivity, aggression, arrogance, dominance

5= Life Lessons, Life Choices, Life Decisions, personal freedom, being courageous, natural flair, courage, non-attachment, utilize learned experiences, variety, adaptability, versatility, understanding, release, surrender, story-telling, mercy, kindness, sympathy

Negative patterns= being rash, irresponsible, inconsistent, unreliability, thoughtlessness, inability to commit, fear of change, rigid in thought and action, stagnate, upheavals and discordant (the number 5 is repeated twice in Anger which increases its vibration and intensifies its presence)

7= Collective Consciousness, spirituality, spiritual awakening, Awareness through spiritual enlightenment and Acceptance, Development, understanding of others, peaceful, poised, inner fortitude, endurance, perseverance, persistence, ability to withstand difficult challenges, NON-CONFORMIST, keen discernment abilities, Trend setter (Ahead of the times)

Negative patterns= Depression, inactivity, hypercritical, anti-social, pessimistic, argumentative, resentful, non-cooperative (7 is also repeated twice in Anger which increases its vibration and intensifies its presence)

9= Universal Love, strength of character, Positive Role Model, Responsible, Empathy and Sympathy, Views things from a higher perspective, Magnetic personality, NON-CONFORMIST, Expansive viewpoint, Effective communicator, Influential, Willing to forgive, Compassionate, Learning to say 'No', Integrity and Wisdom, Understands cycles, New Beginnings

Negative patterns= disconnection, lethargy, inability to concentrate, lack of focus (9 appears twice in anger, therefore its vibration and presence is intensified)

2= Service, Duty, balance, harmony, diplomacy, co-operation, consideration, friendliness, receptivity, Love, Understanding, Personal will, Peace-Maker, Just and Justice, caution, flexibility, happiness, encouragement, Trust

Negative patterns= Indifferent, irresponsible, fearful, pessimism, insensitivity, lack of being considerate, unemotional, unloving, argumentative, disagreeable, fears sudden changes, hate making mistakes, fear of being alone and the unknown

Now, let us listen to what each glyph (letter) is communicating to us.

Again, the vowels are the secret weapons of power in all languages. They are the elementals-Ether, Air, Fire, Water, and Earth. The word 'emotion' literally means 'energies in motion'. Think of them functioning chemically when combining air with fire, water with earth, fire and earth, water and air (wind), earth and air (wind), etc. Each one produces movement and the consonants are the variables that enhance their movements or motions within our personalities. Natural nature is our best example of these natural forces in action. What each of us must remember is that we are the human reflections of the natural forces in nature. Our greatest advantages as human beings are that we can learn to control our 'Inner-G's in motion (emotions)'.

Understanding the Language of our Emotions

A

The Parent of All elements is the vowel Aether.

Aether (Greek: αἰθήρ *aithēr*), also spelled **æther** or **ether.** Our most ancient ancestors before Greece even existed understood 'Aether' as the quintessential element of 'pure air' that is breathed out by the Gods/Goddesses to fill up the various levels beyond terrestrial atmospheres.

Example: Mountains that are thousands of feet high above sea level is thought to be very 'aetheric' in scientific fields of study because the air gets extremely thin the higher up one travels. Astronauts have to wear highly engineered suits to withstand the air that exists above our known concepts of gravity outside of our known atmosphere.

Scientifically, it is the translucent material that fills up the unseen spaces of all 'Omni-verses, Uni-verses', also both celestial and terrestrial spheres (Cosmology). Scientists believe it to be purer than the air breathed by humans. Some are discussing theories about the possibilities of a 'Luminous Aether' existing. Early 19th century physicists also hypothesized that 'Aether' also has something to do with the way light is able to travel through nothingness, void, and spaces that completely lack matter. All elements have directions that they can move in. Aether moves in natural circular motions. It provides suitable atmospheres for all other forces or elements to exist. In the beginning, Aether known as the 'Fifth Element', because of its ability to move in circular motions whereas terrestrial spheres move linearly, scientists promoted it and renamed it as the 'First Element'.

The essential personalities of the vowel 'A' denote elevated wisdom and heightened intuition when utilizing its positive energies. Its image esoterically can link one's mind to the source of divine unity. Instead of allowing our emotional energies to become chaotic while we are in a hypersensitive mind state, the core principle of this vowel encourages us ambitiously to pursue the facts within all disturbing events. It is an established fact that when we are upset or angry we can become easily hurt, emotionally. Our mind states are so hypersensitive during these turbulent moments that we express ourselves improperly. We can avoid these seemingly natural reactions if we have an understanding of the language of emotions and numerology.

Some of the positive and negative elemental personalities of the quintessential vowel 'A' are as follows:

Positive	Negative
• objective	• hypersensitive
• methodical	• impatient
• intellectual	• scattered
• seeks facts	• impractical
• goal oriented	• lacks committal
• creative	• sarcastic
• visionary	• contemptuous

Remember, vowels are the true invisible Overseers, true scientific and spiritual Watchers of all human languages spoken on this planet. They are the records and witnesses of everything thought, and spoken. The other feature of the master vowel 'A' is that it also magnifies all other vowels personalities, energetically. What this means is that it will heighten any emotional state that we are in if it is included as a letter in our emotional states of being.

Therefore, in the emotional orchestrator of scattered emotions, 'Anger' we find the other elemental personality in the image of the letter 'E'.

-E-

I constantly move through space as Air

Some call me the Wind

I Am the element associated with the tfItfD

Truly, if perception is everything, then it's no wonder that the word 'perception' has two 'Es', and is one of the core personalities of the vowel 'E'. It is also the motivator and instigator of action after it receives behavioral ideas from the mind (mental). As an instigator of action, it also carries with it the ability to transform rational behavior into irrational actions. What gives it its ability to affect every level of our human reactions is due to the three horizontal lines associated with its image. Let us dissect it in order to gain a much more profound perspective and elevated perspicacity for this glyph.

When writing this glyph, immediately we must first draw a vertical line. While in the act of drawing this first vertical character, we are simultaneously covering three separate, connecting collective levels of existence:

The above concept

- Top
- middle
- and bottom

As it is Above-It is Below

The below concept

Simultaneously, we are duplicating the same method above with the exception that these three lines are horizontal. The other noticeable quality about these three lines is they are not of the equal proportion. The top line connects at the *spiritual* level, the middle line connects at the *mental* level, and lastly the final line connects at the *physical* level. From this perspective, universal consciousness becomes the central theme of this glyph. Instead of turmoil, harmony becomes another potential outcome, if that is the motivating mindset of each individual when properly controlled.

The mental line is the gateway through which all must pass when accessing the potential benefits of properly drawing on one's spiritual inner strength to manifest well-balanced actions on a physical level. Our actions at any time are always based on various perceptions of occurring events happening in our lives.

Past-present-Future

How we act when we are angry will transform our lives, concretely either for the good or bad. Decisions made while we are angry, in one swift motion will alter our lives. Therefore, we must always think before we 'Act'.

Below are more emerging, merging, mixing, as well as blending emotional energies to consider when ceased with 'anger'.

smart-thinker~hypocritical~intuitive~untrustworthy~innovative~unsettled~

logical~combative~tenacious~parochial~charismatic~corrupt~accomplished~

intolerant~esoterical~irritable~determined~sanctimonious~capable~skittish~

You Can Control Your Inner-Gs in Motion

known as Emotions

NUMBERS HAVE A LANGUAGE OF THEIR OWN

DO THE MATH

When we are working with the esoteric sciences of numerology, we are dealing with the primary constructs of all living forms. Furthermore, LIFE IS AWAKENED by applying the sciences of numerology to everything that is happening around us especially our emotions through word association.

For example, let us consider the word "Something". What our ears really are hearing is "Sum thing". Could it be the sum of individual parts we call things? Those things when combined together mathematically referred to as the "sum total and when we root the sum total of the things, the last part of the sum total is the "Total".

1+2+3+4 is the things. The sum total of these things equals 10. However, we must root the sum total to arrive at our final destination to discover the total of the sum of the things we commonly refer to as "sum thing".

Therefore, 1+0=1 and this would be the Total of all previous mathematical processes. Now we truly know the total of "sum things becoming something". To benefit from the information offered in this book, a dimensional shift must take place in all of our minds. By redefining our deepest fears through the usage of numerology, we can embrace our life's lessons with courage.

Now that we have done the groundwork, it is up to you the reader to utilize both the numeric and alphabetical interpretations using the remaining pages as your personal workbook, and journal to **g**et **r**eal **i**nformation to **e**liminate all of your **f**ear-based emotions.

Happy healing everyone because "LIFE IS STILL WORTH LIV-ING!"

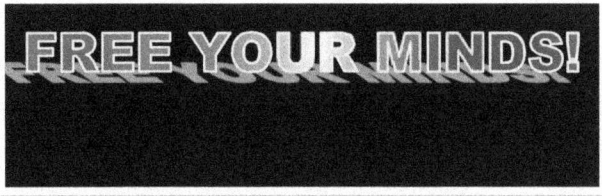

NUMERIC INTERPRETATIONS

LET THE NUMBERS DO THE TALKING

0: Inner gifts, Sensitivity, Strength, Expressiveness, Intuition, Uncertainties

1: New Beginnings, Creativity/Confidence, Awareness of our thoughts, Initiative

2: Decisions, Free Choice, Duality, Service/Duty, Love/Willingness, Trust/Faith

3: Moves other things without changing itself, Catalyst, Leadership, Optimism/Joy, Inspiration, Growth/Abundance, Sensitivity/Expression

4: Community, Foundations, Patience, Determination, Inner-Wisdom, Loyalty, Realistic Values, Self-Control, Stability/Ability, Passion/Persistence

5: Change, Relationships, Freedom/Discipline, Adventures, Life Lessons, Empathy/Sympathy, Resourcefulness, Understanding, Sociability, Kindness, Magnetism, Letting Go

6: Harmony, Unconditional Love, Home/Family, Peace/Peacefulness, Reliability, Humanitarian, Problem Solver, Musical Talent

7: Spirituality, Trust/Openness, Healing, Collective Consciousness, Inner-Strength, Inventor, Acceptance, Spiritual Awakening, Peace, Thoughtfulness

8: Abundance, Ability to Manifest, Personal Power, Success, Inner-Strength, Good Judgment, Discernment, Reciprocity, Dependability, Self-Reliant, Compassion

9: Active Completion, Endings/New Beginnings, Spiritual Awakening, Universal Love, Service to Humanity, Strength of Character, Integrity/Wisdom, Setting Limitations, Humanitarianism, Generosity, Selflessness, Empathy

Remember, if the Total of any word relating to your fears, joys, or whatever you are redefining numerically is a 10, it is really a 1 because 1+0=1=Leadership, Optimism, Confidence Success, and Creative Abilities. The presence of the '0' increases the opportunities to easily access and apply these qualities to one's life.

Certain double numbers are what we call *"Master Vibrations"*. They are not to be rooted. They are heightened vibrations of their single number identity as well as the single number living within them. The number 11 for example has the personality of a heightened (intensified) 2 because 1+1=2, etc.

11: Be aware of your thoughts, Spiritual Enlightenment, Connect with your Higher Self, Idealism, Inspiration, Intuition, Illumination, Visionary, Creativity, Highly Energetic, Helping to raise Spiritual Awareness, Universal Unity

22: Your soul's mission and purpose, Diplomatic, Balance/Harmony,Partnerships/Relationships, Philanthropist, Service/Duty, Peacefulness in all areas of one's life, Devotion, Inner-Wisdom, Realization of the Divine Self

33: Expansion, Spontaneity with Discipline, Broad-mindedness, Encouragement, Clarity, Self-Expression, Talented/Skillful, Energies of the Ascended Masters, Patience

44: Metamorphosis, Reformation of the Self, Acceleration/Ease, Catalytic Motion, Support/Stability amplified, Energies of the Divine Overseers, Establishing Solid Foundations, Be Aware of your intuition, Inner Wisdom amplified

55: Absolute precision to life's experiences, Beneficial Construction, Strategic Methods, Amplification/Reinforcement,

Versatility, Adventure, Curiosities, Releasing Old Habits, Life Lessons, Wonderful New Opportunities, Faces Challenges, Freedom/Discipline Amplified

66: Sacred Orders Celestial/Terrestrial, Divine Order of Personal Life, Higher Concepts of Organization, Systematic Resolutions, Implementations, Amplification of Vision/Acceptance, Amplification of Universal Love/Harmony, Service to Others, Gratitude, Healing, Trust the Universe, Support from Higher Beings

77: Transcendence, Limitless energies to create, Spiritual Advancements, Understands the Consummation of Heaven/Earth, Universal Gate Keeper, Inner Wisdom, Understands Others Intuitively, Tenacious, Follows Divine Guidance, Empathic, and Education

88: Elevation/Recognition, Limitless Consciousness, Elevation of Knowing, Prophetic Understanding, Master Guide of Implementations, Boundless capabilities, Compassionate, Sensitive to subtle energies, Business Acumen, Conscious usage of Power to Manifest Abundance, Self-Discipline, Patience, Practicality, Dependability, Ambition, Heightened Abilities of Discernment, Inner-Wisdom, Progress/Attainment

99: Supreme Cycles, Evolution/Revolution, Divine Comprehension of All Paths, Flexibility, Integrity/Wisdom on every level, Supreme Unifier, Divine Seer ship, Charismatic, Leadership,

Conclusions/New Beginnings, Universal Spiritual Laws, Humanitarianism, Supreme Healer, Fear not that old things are ending, Supreme Optimism

*Please be aware that the higher these numbers go (triplicity, etc) the vibration continues to become extremely concentrated *

Listen to the Numbers

What do they hear?

Alphabetic Interpretations

Understanding the Language of Letters

A   Divine Unity, Enlightened Consciousness, Transformation through Proper Expression, Truth, Ambition, Unifier between God/Humanity, Preeminent Intelligence, Mystical Utterance/Breath

B   Focused Abilities of Expression, Heightened Intellect, Fertility/Growth, Productive/Creative

C   Creative Force of Spoken Word, Aware of Rhythms/Cycles, Androgynous, Idealistic

D Magnetism on All levels, Fertility, Instinctual Discernment, Masters of Love, Producers of great joy/abundance

E Universal Consciousness, Divine Ideas, Elevation of Intuition, Creator of Harmony, Self-Transformation, Perception, Clairaudience, Communication on Higher Levels

F Enterprising attainment methods using Harmony, Innate Optimism, Liveliness, Charismatic, Influential

G Memory, Patience, Perseverance, Spiritual Energy, Learning the proper use of the Sex Force, Gifts of Knowing, Acumen

H Master of Communication, Imagination, Intuition, New birth of expressions, Creative Feminine Force, New Life/Opportunities

I Divine Love, Transmutation, Unifier of Heart/Mind, Self-Sufficient, Memory, Metaphysical Insights, Activator, Manifesting, Compassion, Strengthener

J Enthusiasm, Optimism, Reaper of Cosmic Love, Hidden potentials, Pioneering, Must love what they do, Generous

K New Beginnings, Creativity, Active Mind, Inspirational on all levels, Love to Love, Spiritual Awakening of Humanity

L Magnetism on All Levels, Feminine Energies, Intuitive, Receptivity, Spirituality, Intellectual/Artistic, Must control Feminine Energies

M Primal, Regeneration, Feminine Energy of Creation, Hidden Abilities, Abilities to Master Emotions, Divine Consciousness, Highly Intuitive

N Intentional Transmutation, Fertility, Inexhaustible Life-Forces, Processes of Controlled Change, Keen sense of smell, Developing Spiritual Discernment, Ecstasy, See/work with Auras, Protective, Loyal

O Harmony, Justice, Balance, Intuition, Feminine Energies, Receptivity, Spiritual Judgment, Security, Success, Focused Visualization, Fearful of Failure, Karmic

P Master of Storytelling, Mastery over Hidden Expressions, Poetic, Great Writers, Longs for Spiritual Progress

Q Activates Intuitive Centers, Abundance in Joy/Harmony, Egyptian Mysteries, Unifier of Mind/Heart, Intelligent Reasoning, Unity/Aspiration, Healer, Gifts of Manifestation, Strong Imaginations, Optimism, Selflessness, Initiations

R Master Builder of Love/Wisdom/Spiritual Transformation, Inspiration on Higher Levels, Great Intellectuals, Elevated abilities of Discernment, Healing

S Serpent Mysteries, Instincts, Trust, Personal Evolution, Symbol of Eternity, Clairvoyance, Wisdom, Prophetic, Healing, Maximum Mobility, Masters of Transmutation

T Honor, Dignity, Spiritual Warriorship, Self-Mastery, Courage, Aspirations, Feminine Intuition, Astral magic, Sympathetic, Inspirational Universal Love

U Strong Intuition, Tenacious, Reliable, Protective, Visionary, Practical, Creative Expression, Patient, Gentle, Birth Giving, Illumination/Inspiration, Connections to the Earth, Excellent Judges of Character, Conservative

V Openness, Fruitfulness, Lover of Life's bounty, Unifier, Love for the Arts, Excellent Judge of Character, Perseverance, Rewards, Desires Liberation, Creative, Compassionate, Kindness, Sexual Forces that must be controlled

W Unites Love/Intuition/Cycles, Strong Emotions, Must learn to move through change, Strong Artistic Abilities, Must learn to prevent depression

X Philosopher, Lover of the Arts, Mediator of Higher Knowledge, Sexual Magic, Primal forces, Family/Friends, Archetypal forces of creation, Ancient Mysteries, Astral Travel

Y Transmutation on the highest level, Profound Intuition/Aspiration, Imitator, Abilities to understand the creative process, Understands origins, Awakens the Spiritual Child within, Androgynous

Z Electrical, Primal, Intuitive Knowledge, Double-edged, Quick, Hates Delays, Discrimination on Higher Levels, Spiritual consciousness, Physical Consciousness, Occultism, Highly Intellectual, Loves Foreign Languages, Adaptable, Genius, Alchemy

CH Higher Vision, Must learn how to balance, Self-imposed limitations, Purity/Clarity of Purpose, Understands the cycles/rhythms of life

PH Transformation/Initiation, Lover of all things Ancient, Pathway to regeneration, Involution/Evolution, Seeker of Truth, Agents of Great Evolutionary Change

SH Activation of Primal Transmutation, Must maintain Emotional Balance, Naturally Enlightened, Instinctual Spirituality, Helpers of Humanity

TH Openers of the Cosmic Gateways, Karmic, Learning to be Responsible, Out of body experiences, Must control intuitive instincts, Mobility to go to higher levels

TZ Intuition, Creative Imaginations, Intolerance, Teachers, Visionaries

Letters are Powerful Communicators

Decode All Fear Based Emotions

Letter and Number Formula

1	2	3	4	5	6	7	8	9
A	B	C	D	E	F	G	H	I
J	K	L	M	N	O	P	Q	R
S	T	U	V	W	X	Y	Z	

***Remember to match each letter to its number. You can multiply and add to see if you get different insights-It's Fun! Just do not split Master Numbers. The key is to examine each number separately in order to understand the different levels of each fear based emotion. Then look for repetitious numbers that might show up in that particular fear because then it intensifies its presence. Examine its individual numbers.

Then examine the sum total as well before examining the final summation. Afterwards, look at the interpretations for each letter and write down what message that particular fear based emotion is trying to communicate to you.***

Remember
GRIEF means . . .
Getting **R**eal **I**nformation

Eliminates **F**ear

Journal Pages
"A Healing Must Take Place"

Journal Pages
"A Healing Must Take Place"
Decode Your Fear Based Emotions on These Pages

Journal Pages
"A Healing Must Take Place"
Decode Your Fear Based Emotions on These Pages

Journal Pages
"A Healing Must Take Place"
Decode Your Fear Based Emotions on These Pages

Journal Pages
"A Healing Must Take Place"
Decode Your Fear Based Emotions on These Pages

Journal Pages
"A Healing Must Take Place"
Decode Your Fear Based Emotions on These Pages

Journal Pages
"A Healing Must Take Place"
Decode Your Fear Based Emotions on These Pages

Journal Pages
"A Healing Must Take Place"
Decode Your Fear Based Emotions on These Pages

Journal Pages
"A Healing Must Take Place"
Decode Your Fear Based Emotions on These Pages

Journal Pages
"A Healing Must Take Place"
Decode Your Fear Based Emotions on These Pages

Journal Pages
"A Healing Must Take Place"
Decode Your Fear Based Emotions on These Pages

Journal Pages
"A Healing Must Take Place"
Decode Your Fear Based Emotions on These Pages

Journal Pages
"A Healing Must Take Place"
Decode Your Fear Based Emotions on These Pages

Journal Pages
"A Healing Must Take Place"
Decode Your Fear Based Emotions on These Pages

Journal Pages
"A Healing Must Take Place"
Decode Your Fear Based Emotions on These Pages

Journal Pages
"A Healing Must Take Place"
Decode Your Fear Based Emotions on These Pages

Journal Pages
"A Healing Must Take Place"
Decode Your Fear Based Emotions on These Pages

Journal Pages
"A Healing Must Take Place"
Decode Your Fear Based Emotions on These Pages

Journal Pages
"A Healing Must Take Place"
Decode Your Fear Based Emotions on These Pages

Journal Pages
"A Healing Must Take Place"
Decode Your Fear Based Emotions on These Pages

Journal Pages
"A Healing Must Take Place"
Decode Your Fear Based Emotions on These Pages

Journal Pages
"A Healing Must Take Place"
Decode Your Fear Based Emotions on These Pages

Journal Pages
"A Healing Must Take Place"
Decode Your Fear Based Emotions on These Pages

Journal Pages
"A Healing Must Take Place"
Decode Your Fear Based Emotions on These Pages

Journal Pages
"A Healing Must Take Place"
Decode Your Fear Based Emotions on These Pages
REFERENCES

Andrews, Ted. *The magical name: a practical technique for inner power.* Llewellyn Publications, 1991.

"Em Hotep - Egyptology for the Layperson and the Scholar." *Dmninf*, www.ntviser.net/www.emhotep.net.

Ocran, York Z. K. Malachi, "Actual Fact 17: Emotional Energy". UNW Publications, Print Date Unknown

"Sacred Scribes Joanne Walmsley." *ANGEL NUMBERS*, sacredscribes.blogspot.com/p/angel-numbers.html.

Journal Pages
"A Healing Must Take Place"
Decode Your Fear Based Emotions on These Pages

ACKNOWLEDGEMENTS

I thank my Celestial and Terrestrial parents most of All.

My two driving forces that constantly propel me to seek out answers to various information is my daughter and my grandson, who from time to time call upon me to answer things that they are challenged with-Thank you.

Thank you to all of my amazing God-Children.

Many thanks to all of my wonderful Master Teachers from all walks of theologies and philosophies.

One of my strongest Master Teachers remains to be H.E. Dr. Malachi York, who strongly said, "You all are going to have to learn to do the math".

Thank you to all of my wonderful family and friends who constantly act as powerful support system.

Thank you to the Muzikical Voice for the Freedom of Dr. York, Bro. Ntelek 9.

Thank you Lynda Mosley, owner of Natures Treasures for blessing me to work around many wonderful elemental teaching tools.

Thank you, Robert "White Eagle" Browning (RIP). Keep soaring high above us- A-HO!

I thank all of humanity, who just might find that the information presented in this format will give them a better way to have understanding of all things facing them, in a numerical paradigm.

Journal Pages
"A Healing Must Take Place"
Decode Your Fear Based Emotions on These Pages

ABOUT THE AUTHOR

Net-Hetep Ta'Nesert is the Chief Grief Originist at HOST. The acronym stands for Healing OurSelves Together. She is also the author of the inspirational non-fiction, "Facing the Beast In Love's Honor by Rainbow © Publish America". She has been studying numerology for more than a decade.

As a new concept leader in redefining what healthy grief resolutions resembles, she provides correct information and resources for grieving individuals who have lost loved ones through death or any other traumatic situations.

Her approach, although orthodox is to share meaningful information that is esoteric in its nature.

The information she shares reveals deeper concepts meant to awaken the spiritual, scientific, and sound right reasoning faculties latent within the human mind.

Her approach covers both the traditional and alternative suggestions related holistically to humanity's well-being.

Her heart driven intention is to provide and guide humanity towards lasting, healing results after experiencing life's sudden and traumatic encounters. Her mission is to share caring and useful information that guides humanity to the resources to feel whole and secure again.

Journal Pages
"A Healing Must Take Place"
Decode Your Fear Based Emotions on These Pages

She states, "Commitment and motivation towards humanity, and our planet is focused on this one healing reality - Life is still worth living!"